This life is not the only one we live. We live more lives
concurrently.
And the world in which we live this life is not the only one.

Time and space and our understanding of both are not all that
exist but only what our given capabilities enable us to perceive.

We live other lives concurrently with this one, at the same age
and at different ages.

Something which happens to us here does not necessarily
happen to us elsewhere or it may happen but differently.

We are born here, we live and die here, but in other places we
continue to live because our death did not happen. Those who
knew us witness our passing, but elsewhere we are not aware
and neither are they that something happened to us. Our lives
continue as if nothing happened because what happens here
does not happen everywhere.

We have lives with different scenarios. What there is here is only
real in the narrow concept of here and not all there is in the wider
context.

How many other lives, how many worlds? It is all beyond numbers, beyond measurements of time or space or size or quantity or anything at all of what we are accustomed to and use here.

Limitless.

By design and not accidentally, no big bangs, we exist.

We never die as we move seamlessly from one world or bubble to another. No bang, however big, no world war, no errand asteroid, no catastrophic disaster of any description, can affect any other bubble but the one we live in and know. Our world, our bubble, can end just like we die and we would not know it anywhere else. We never end and our broader world never ends either.

By design.

We are limited in our understanding of our Creator and the motives, purpose and objectives which led to us being where we are.

As if such motives, purpose and objectives must necessarily exist or that, even if they did, we could or should be capable of understanding them.

This is our time span but not the only one in all realities. All and everything are concurrent. All of the past, all of the present, all of the future, all of eternity.

Many of us believe that our deceased ancestors watch over us and that they even sometimes protect us.

Not so. They are not aware of our reality, which is the bubble they left behind.

Death is an event to people who know us or of us here but not to us, nowhere are we aware that we died somewhere in our other bubbles. In them we continue as we were and with the same reality continuing.

Our sins and transgressions may not have happened in our other lives or they happened differently and with different outcomes.

What we did to others, what others did to us, all are punished or rewarded in our other bubbles and that is also by design.

Which leaves our perceptions of God and morality, of right and wrong, of good and evil, of crime and punishment, of a reward for a virtuous life, intact, only not as we think them.

To think of how long we live in this life we must use time as our reference point, but time does not exist beyond our bubbles. We are five years old or eighteen or thirty concurrently, with no time reference points, no limits. We are forever.

By design.

We are not aware of our other lives in other bubbles and no scientific advancement can enable us to know. Our Science, our laws of Physics, the Chemical elements, are of and for this and other bubbles, but not for all. Other, different tools exist in other bubbles which are just as valid and as real as ours are to us here.

In this bubble where we live we have our laws of nature and of Physics which govern us.

We also have our universe and the planets and the stars which are exclusively ours, of this same bubble, although other such do exist and not somewhere else or at another time, the next bubble is not a kilometre, a metre, a centimetre away, it is also here and now.

All living things and not just us humans follow the same path, never dying, just moving from one bubble to another and another and another, just as we do.

And we have a History, but other bubbles have different Histories, events in our History either did not happen at all or they happened differently.

Unidentified flying objects or UFOs and aliens are not crossovers from other bubbles, accidental or not. There is never any physical cross-over from one bubble to another. All unexplained or strange phenomena are of this bubble and this bubble only.

In our other bubbles we have variances in our personality, physical characteristics and the paths our lives take.

Those who did not have children in this bubble, in others they do. Miscarriages did not happen, those unborn children were born.

Similarly, sicknesses did not happen as they happened here. We live many lives. Misfortune and hardship here, not so elsewhere and it is our deeds in one bubble which determine the quality of our lives in other.

We are entities of physical manifestations and the worlds or bubbles we live in have their own physical manifestations too.

How many? How many worlds, how many bubbles? We seek to attach numbers to everything to better understand but precisely the point is that we may be able to understand far better without the use of or the need for numbers.

We seek to reach the stars and to explore our universe, we send rockets and spaceships, but wherever we may reach we will still be only in our own bubble, inescapably.

By design.

Our Creator is in a world of no beginning, that is, of no time frames. Our world, our bubble, all the bubbles, were created millions of years ago or two seconds ago. There is no time beyond our bubbles, no numbers, no need for measuring anything. It is a world beyond the measured or the measurable.

We are a wholly self regulated assemblance of worlds which, once created, require no further intervention by our Creator. All of our worlds' needs, physical, spiritual or moral are self contained.

And self regulated.

By design.

We believe our world to be a physical world, made of solid matter, but if other worlds coexist concurrently and are occupying the same space and all those other worlds are similarly self contained, self regulated and are similarly physical too, how solid or physical can our solidity and physicality be?

In the grandest of all the grand schemes of all reality neither we nor everything we can reach or sense around us are physical but merely perceptions.

Our idea of what space is cannot describe or explain the spacial relation among the bubbles. They are not separate in the sense that there is a here and a there, something happens here and something else happens there. They are all together, coexisting, entwined, overlapping, with different scenarios being enacted continuously and we are never aware of perpetually moving from one to the other and the other and the other living all our lives contemporaneously.

We die and everyone in this bubble may imagine it but in reality we carry on, maybe at a younger age or maybe not, or rather different situations continue and in them we are never aware that we left one bubble, only that our lives in our other bubbles are good or not so good, in accordance to our deeds in the bubble we left behind.

By design.

The good is rewarded, the bad is punished, a moral dimension does exist and it may be the purpose of it all.

Our worlds were created in our Creator's world's own image: No space, no time, no beginning and no end.

And evolution? The Neanderthals? The Ice Age? The origin of Man?

Yes, all happened in this world as we imagine it, but in other worlds they were already beyond those stages or such stages never existed.

Our Creator is in a world of no beginning and no end, time is non existent and completely irrelevant, as are also numbers, since there is no need for measuring.

It is why the question of the origin of our Creator or who then created our Creator does not arise.

The worlds and universes in which we live are completely self regulated with no puppeteer pulling any strings. Everything in them, the good, the bad, the crime and the punishment, the morality and the dispensing of justice, are self regulated.

Beyond our bubbles, in the world which created us, there is no need for numbers, for Mathematics, for Physics, for Chemistry. Our world and all the other worlds or bubbles were created in the image of the world of our Creator with no parameters of time or space and of beginning or end. The times we think we passed are still present somewhere and so are we in them and the people we knew, nothing disappears, nothing ends.

We are eternal in the sense that we do not end, eternal being a wrong term as it is difficult to escape the terminology of what we have and know here and view everything from outside, from outside all our bubbles, "all" being yet another trap as it implies something finite. There is no all and no eternal and no absolutes of anything. We are in shackles by numbers even in ways we are not conscious of and we cannot perceive a world without them, but that is where the real reality is.

We believe we are of solid matter and everything around us is solid matter too, it has volume which we can measure, nothing can possibly coexist in the same space that we inhabit. Why? Because nothing can be where we are since we do not bump into it.

As numbers do not exist beyond our worlds, in the world of our Creator, the oneness or not of our Creator cannot be considered. All that we may know is that we and our worlds were created and there was an act of creation. Created to be indestructible because we and our worlds were not made of destructible matter.

There are no portals which may lead to other worlds beyond our own. Everything is of and for this world only.

Everything in our world and worlds is wholly self regulated, with punishment or forgiveness of our sins and our trespassed possible through true remorse and repentance constantly and instantaneously effected.

By design.

There is no Day of Judgment, judgment is continuously and unfailingly carried out.

No Heaven in some post death Elysian Fields and no Hell in a grim punishing Hades. All is here in our never ending lives.

Beyond our worlds are worlds and a limitless universe of no matter, no matter of any earthlese description, nothing solid as we understand it, no time, no space, no Mathematics, no Laws of Physics, no past, no present, no future, only limitless eternity and that is the world of our Creator, one limitless vastness beyond what we know or can understand.

In that world there are other ways, other kinds of matter which our laws of Physics here cannot account for as they apply only to our world and not in the world of our Creator.

Our limitless worlds or bubbles are all part of the same world, one world, but separate from each other, all one, all apart.

As it is in our Creator's world, not one, not solid, not aetherial or spiritual, a world beyond our comprehension, a world just like our own in its constitution if not its content, we are in our Creator's world's own image.

The use of the singular form for our Creator is not intended to be literal. In our Creator's world of no numbers the singular and the plural do not exist.

Take one person in our world of bubbles. One person? But the same person is existing in limitless worlds. Singular or plural then for that person?

The bubbles are not parallel, as in parallel universes, side by side. They all coexist with our concept of space not valid in the overall reality, just as our concept of physicality is not valid either. We imagine a lot of what we perceive to be true or real because this is how we are, it is a measure of our limitations.

No Heaven and Hell and no Day of Judgment does not mean impunity for sins, transgressions or misdemeanors and no reward for living a good and virtuous life.

Justice for good and evil and for all good and all bad is served instantaneously and not only in one but in many bubbles and the degree of the punishment or reward is directly determined by the degree of the good and the bad of our deeds.

The life we live in any one bubble is in complete accordance to our deeds elsewhere. It is a world created thus.

By design.

In the world beyond our own worlds, where there are no numbers and no measurements of anything at all, there is no good and evil. Justice is effected, not on the basis of good or bad, but on the basis of like begets like.

What we do, be it good or bad, will be what shall be done also to ourselves, in different ways but on the same level. No reward for good or punishment for bad, but simply like for like.

It is so for everything we do in all our lives in all our worlds, we reap what we sow exactly.

By design.

There is no rule that all our worlds necessarily share the same sky or the same universe. What we look up in the sky is exclusively of our world, even if other worlds in our world of worlds may be looking up at the same sky.

It is why speculated mishaps like asteroid collisions or alien invasions would affect only this world and no other, unless another has the same or similar scenario.

And therein lies the reason why our worlds, and we in them, are indestructible.

By design.

Neither the world beyond our worlds nor the Creator of our worlds and of ourselves were created themselves. That would have necessitated a point in time when they did not exist and then they came into being, so there would have been an act of Creation.

But in a world beyond time and measurements, where time does not exist not even as a concept, such a point cannot exist.

We do not die. We simply continue to live elsewhere at different ages.

We are also born elsewhere limitless times. Our physical characteristics after we are born are determined by genetic inheritance which may also determine more than our physical appearance, but our personality is, to a large extent, the same in all our lives, we are the same persons but with variances.

The kind of parents or family we have, the kind of place we are at with respect of peace and comfort, the directions our lives take, are all determined by our deeds elsewhere. All are as punishment or reward, all a result of justice served and all are self regulated, all flowing through and there can be no avoidance of anything at all.

By design.

We keep moving from one world to another without ever knowing it, not when we die but at all times, living all our lives in a non time governed reality.

We take one decision from two or more options. In another world we took another decision. Or another. Or another.

A near mishap almost happened to us and we think we had a lucky escape, but not so in all our lives. Limitless scenarios are continuously being played out in our limitless lives in our limitless worlds and all this by design.

There is no continuation of our lives elsewhere in terms of a different place, there is no there or here, just as there is no past or present, all space is limitless and so is all time and neither is subject to oneness or plurality.

Same as our Creator who is not subject to oneness or plurality or can be defined by age or gender.

Our limitless world of worlds was a result of an Act of Creation but there was no such act for the world of our Creator or for our Creator, neither was created.